Weather Wise

Wind

Helen Cox Cannons

Raintree is an imprint of Capstone Global Library Limited, a company incorporated in England and Wales having its registered office at 7 Pilgrim Street, London, EC4V 6LB – Registered company number: 6695582

www.raintreepublishers.co.uk
myorders@raintreepublishers.co.uk

Text © Capstone Global Library Limited 2015
First published in hardback in 2014
The moral rights of the proprietor have been asserted.

Edited by Siân Smith and John-Paul Wilkins
Designed by Philippa Jenkins
Picture research by Ruth Blair
Production by Victoria Fitzgerald
Originated by Capstone Global Library Ltd
Printed and bound in China

ISBN 978 1 4062 8482 9
18 17 16 15 14
10 9 8 7 6 5 4 3 2 1

British Library Cataloguing in Publication Data
A full catalogue record for this book is available from the British Library.

Acknowledgements
We would like to thank the following for permission to reproduce photographs: Alamy: Super Nova Images, 19; Dreamstime: Reb, 8; Getty Images: Joe Raedle, cover; iStockphoto: invictus999, 4, MarcusPhoto1, 10, Opla, 11; NASA: 18, 23 (middle); Shutterstock: andreiuc88, 13, Andrew Zarivny, 22, Felix Mizioznikov, 6, Fer Gregory, 16, 23 (bottom), Hallgerd, 21, Joel Calheiros, 9, jukurae, 14, Martin Haas, 17, S. Borisov, 12, Sundraw Photography, 20, Vita Khorzhevska, 5, 23 (top), Zloneg, 7.

We would like to thank John Horel for his invaluable help in the preparation of this book.

Every effort has been made to contact copyright holders of material reproduced in this book. Any omissions will be rectified in subsequent printings if notice is given to the publisher.

Contents

What is wind?

Wind is moving air.

Wind moves in many **directions**.

You can feel wind on your body.

Wind moves things around.

Wind moves across the land.

Wind moves across the oceans.

Wind can be gentle. A gentle wind is called a breeze.

Wind can be strong. A strong
wind is called a gale.

What does wind do?

Wind moves air around the world. Wind can bring warm air in the summer.

Wind can bring cold air in the winter.

Types of wind

Some winds change direction every day. Winds in the mountains change direction a lot.

14

Some winds blow in the same
direction for a long time.

Wild winds

A **tornado** is a spinning tube of air. It touches both the clouds and the ground.

A tornado is sometimes called a twister. It is so strong that it can pull up trees and tear down houses.

eye

A **hurricane** starts over a warm ocean and may move toward land. The middle of a hurricane is called the eye.

A hurricane brings very strong winds and rain.

How does wind help us?

Wind can bring rain. Rain helps plants grow.

Wind can be fun!

Did you know?

These are wind turbines. Wind turns the blades of a turbine. This makes electricity to power our homes.

Picture glossary

direction way

hurricane storm with very strong winds

tornado storm with very strong winds that forms a cloud shaped like a funnel

Index

Notes for parents and teachers

Before reading

Assess background knowledge. Ask: What is wind? Are there different kinds of wind?

After reading

Recall and reflection: Ask the children if their ideas about wind at the beginning were correct. What else do they wonder about?

Sentence knowledge: Ask children to look at page 19. How many sentences are on this page? How can they tell?

Word recognition: Ask children to point at the word *moves* on page 7. Can they also find it on page 8?